VALLEY OF THE KINGS

GRAEME RYAN

VALLEY OF THE KINGS

Coverstory books

First published in paperback format by Coverstory books, 2022; 2nd edition 2023

ISBN 978-1-7397660-7-8

Copyright © Graeme Ryan 2023

Cover illustration 'The Falcon Horus' by Jane Gryspeerdt © 2022.

www.coverstorybooks.com

This book is dedicated to Jane - and to the
memory of my mother and father.

(b)

Contents

LONG TIDE

BRIGHT STAR

SEVEN PATHS

LOST-LOVE LETTER

VALLEY OF THE KINGS

✳

LONG TIDE

The Moment

'There is a Moment in each Day that Satan cannot Find, nor can his Watch-Fiends find it…
when it once is found it Renovates every Moment of the Day if rightly placed.'
'Milton Pl 35' William Blake

The earth at night: jewelled cities
  and necklaces of light
    clasping the skin of our world.

Windows with their scimitars of glass
  jump back into completeness
    out of the sword-swallowing air,

fire-hoses gulp themselves back mid-spate,
  flames quench themselves into flarings,
    into sparks of past embers

red as the pulse of standby lights.
  On shorelines of traffic demented sirens
    diminuendo to curlew-calls.

Put away the deadly components -
  stow the knives, bleach and nail-bombs safely in their drawers,
    switch off the blue lights of ambulances,

raise hands in greeting as the headlights
  of cars find a way though time
    before all this ever happened.

Pick up the phone and a message appears:
  'I will shew you all alive the world
    where ev'ry particle of dust breathes forth its joy'.

The moment accelerates into a minute, an hour,
  puts faces back onto heads and people back together;
    swings gates wide onto paths,

turns keys turn in their locks,
     makes missing ones return and all is well.
          Hold tight. Do not blink. Let this be our prayer.

Waters of Life

The first time I drowned
heart and lungs flicked a switch
and I was briefly everywhere,
bladder-wrack popping and sparking,
currents knotting their birth-cords

and winding-sheets. I surged
past shorelines and hospitals,
bobbed up during an ultrasound
then vanished again. What promises
I made in the scour and churn of pebbles

were swallow-dived and back-
-flipped into a treatment plant,
piped through and poured, simple as you like
into a glass of water rocking
prisms of light by the bedside.

The second time I drowned
I tasted the river-pool I was born in,
tried on a suit of current,
touched threads of the sun.
My mother and father swam next to me -

we went through holes in the water
to find the cities of light:
aquifers we never need name
because they are flowing inside us.
Between the first swallow

and the last sip we take
many lifetimes intervene. I just
wish we could have stayed out there longer,
found a way to discover
how the vent meets the source.

Ignition

I put on a suit of light in the ovum,
entered the long tide

saw the faces of my mum and dad become mine,
each wave carrying ancestors with it

sending a flash down each sleeve of night
in electricity of the past and to-come.

Remember the smell of sparks from the wires of the dodgems,
the tang of a struck match, black-dot fumes of a cap gun?

We crept as kids into the garden shed
and dared each other to put the tips of our tongues

on the two-pronged light socket for kicks -
tingled in the after-shock -

sucked a 1901 dark-copper penny
to see if we could time-travel while the sun lasered ants

through a magnifying-glass on the paving slabs.
I don't have my flying dreams so often now

but after my step-dad's funeral I glimpsed a chariot
that seemed to move through clouds as the sun broke

and sometimes I feel I could still pull on the air
like at the edge of a swimming pool,

lift myself up to keep on rising above the roofs
and marram-grass dunes of St Anne's

sensing in the solar plexus
the evening light open pavilions that travel great distances.

But what did it mean that night when the blood-thump
in my heart almost came to a stop?

In the dream I was standing outside our house,
my mother and sister behind me

and I had to go in in order to save us and I couldn't
because death and darkness were going at it hammer and tongs,

waking me bolt upright to grasp each breath.
It was the week after mum died.

My friend John has his own story, a nightmare
that turned into something beating inside his hair

until in the dream he touched it and a bat flew out, bringing peace.
Once on St Anne's beach near the pier there was a jolt in the air

and I smelt the after-shock of the lightning bolt
that just missed me, a singed strand of hair - a sign? -

followed by the bomb-blast overhead and the first big drops.
We listened for thunder on the train track, our ears to the rails,

became both medium and current for the electric eel
at puberty, crossing the rope bridge with its naked lines

as they flashed back and forth in torrential rain,
summoning the girls in their summer frocks.

The leap to the heart that day as she got off the bus,
the smile she had. In my father's house are many mansions:

the current blows the locks like the look she gave me once
arcing through time and space, because the world is dreaming us

beating with wings inside that alight
then take off in new formations.

Arion

The lyre-player saved by dolphins in the Greek myth.
To the memory of J.O'R

Our pod rode the tide,
rounded Inner and Outer Hebrides,
Anglesey, Bryher and Herm,

surfed the Straits of Dover
and headed up Thames
one dawn in a year

when the sun's cockle-shell
opens a hinge between worlds
to gild Chatham and the Isle of Grain.

Then we saw him. What a sea-change
from musician to bobbing manikin:
ripped Cargoes and denim jacket,

rizlas and a wallet of soaked tobacco -
this shapeshifter of the current
who landed from Tower bridge in the dark

with a plectrum in his pocket.
We gathered close and nudged him,
reached out flippers and bore him

past Gravesend and Sheppey,
the first mudlark glimpsing us
as her detector clicked for treasure on the North shore.

We floated him safe onto smooth flanks of mud,
spoke sonar to him
as his mouth gushed with water.

Wordlessly he spoke back to us,
fingers waking to patterns on his Gretsch guitar
(still on its stand in his Battersea flat)

as he found a voice
through jewel-wet eye-lashes
for his voyage -

Satan you freakin' watch-fiend
There's a moment in the day
You cannot find, never find
That blazes on in my mind

A finger of sun touched him,
two cormorants flew past
creaking wings, iridescent.

        Kawasakis speed-bumped the Embankment,
artics, freight trains and jets sprang up
to sand-blast the dawn,

pipes flushed, key-codes beeped
and the cleaners in The Commons
roaring their nozzles

into carpet-pile and clooties of dust
reminded him of factory ships
hoovering Dogger Bank

as they got to work on the front benches.
We plunged deep and set off with him,
steering a course for the Hesperides.

Way-Station on the M4

He spoke from a sugar-spilled table
rubbing coke grains into his gums:

'Slashed by sun-glare through lorry spray,
wiper torn, radio spitting static, *verðuft*,

I unticked the indicator at the last minute,
shunned the junction for Gordano,

sky piling up lead ore behind me
blue radium in front of me

till I reached Almondsbury steaming
in the cloud-burst.

Holding my nerve in middle lane
after lorry-breathing behemoth slow lane

I slalomed out East to the fast lane and its lethal waterslides,
the aquaplaned inquests and dodgem-shunts,

the heart-stopping prayer of a foot hard down
on the brake pedal.

By Leigh Delamere Services I sat down and wept' he said
'for all that my life had become.'

An AA man
was selling sanctuary in the foyer with the eyes of the born-again:

'A faire feeld ful of folk fond I in this wildernesse' he declared

but the red plastic stools of the burger outlet
spun in rigid unbreakability according to the Law

and the metal spatula of the baseball-capped attendant
scraped roadkill off the griddle

and the tanker-driver in his livery
fed machines that beeped and nudged and winked

inanities. By the news-stand the assistant looked kindly
and a wire plugged itself back in, melting typefaces

and headlines on the shelves, so that 'How Dare They! Something
    Must Be Done!'
in *The Mail* became 'Everything that Lives is Holy'

and a celebrity in *The Sun* pronounced
'The cistern contains, the fountain overflows -

How do you know but ev'ry Bird that cuts his airy way
Is an immense world of delight, clos'd by your senses five?'

Then I remembered Volta, discoverer of voltage,
waiting in a van somewhere in a car-park

in this region's traffic network
rarer than a long-billed dowitcher on a shoreline of seagulls.

'By Leigh Delamere Services I sat down and wept' said the stranger
'for all that my life had become,

racing the metalled highways
from Zion to Babylon.'

Behind his eyes was the circuit-breaker inside us all
which had led

to this flooring, these counters, these rustling packets
bar-coded in print-outs of *Lost* and *Missing-in-Action*.

14

'Of all manere of menne, the meene and the riche,
Werchynge and wandrynge as the world asketh

Wherefore gan we meten this marveillous dream?'
said the AA man looking up

as rain-clouds wired their immense electrical circuits
over Membury, Chievely, Reading, Heston, South Mimms.

Sirens of the M25
whirled passengers into way-stations of the lost and found

scrolling through message after message
in the sea-roar.

I followed the man onto the bridge -

he scaled the ledge
over the eight lanes

exchanged a word with the sun
on the arc of a rainbow

and jumped.

The Homeless Man Thinks of Ancient Egypt

I pray to the sun on these temple walls,
the shifting angles and blaze of it,
the way it melts the pavement ice

mid-morning near the cashpoint.
I see merchants, astronomers and viziers
sitting in the window of the coffee-shop opposite -

then they become slaves and slave-owners,
baboons manoeuvring the flow and current
of glinting windscreens.

Tax-collectors snap crocodile heads
to cancel me with an eye-blink;
asps scatter hawks and flocks of chattering ibis.

I am sore beggar and heretic
but Horus shares the sun's strength with everyone
and for moments He lets me stop time

freezing the figures inside KFC and BetFred the Bonus-King,
jamming the screens inside Lloyds Bank
while Ra makes a gong-bath out of the street-roar.

The gas-workers toil in their jack-hammer clatter
on the banks of the traffic-river,
one squeezes the life out of a cigarette,

the vapour of his breath in a shaft of sun
is as mine in the aching air - we are brothers
under this midday moon I take for divination and augury.

The sun's transit takes the blaze
behind high roofs; there is a trapezium of light
I shuffle to at the corner; it forecloses.

Someone has bought me a coffee, her glance contains a smile.
I open the lid, take a careful sip. A packet of crisps too.
The moneylenders have not quite taken over the temple.

Anubis walks up in the likeness of a jackal-headed dog,
just out of reach. Eyes alert, he sniffs me.
Weigher of souls, tomb-guardian, am I fit for Paradise?

Palms

I love this earth he says
as his spade digs a trench for water
in the peach orchard
his grandparents planted
on the wrong side of the peace-

wall as it happens, while the *whumping*
doppler of helicopters
vibrates his breast-bone.
He, sun-struck with dazzle
from the caged windscreens of armoured cars,

the muzzles of guns and razor wire
mirrored in the soldiers' shades.
Their glare welds his
wife and children,
his gap-toothed mother, into
shapes of wrought iron. Look,

goldfinches have flown in
to sip the water he dribbles and spurts
from a hose into the trench,
their calls weightless
as wind-chimes. The turret

of a tank turns through its degrees,
the nostrils of the barrel sniff him
as he leans as to a prayer wheel
grinding a trowel with his palms
into soil that once grew peaches.

A trigger-finger slips.
Killer bees rake the soil.
Blood is a snake
that moves slowly

from here to nowhere.
He is bent over as if kissing the soil.
This last touch of warm grains
holds no laying on,
no laying on of hands or prayer
he can fathom.

To Become A Nightingale

Struck dumb by Universal Credit
I entered the hedge-school of charity shops,
prised apart jackets of musty spinneys on the men's rail
dense with tweed, leather, rayon, polyester
looking for subfusc/olive - found
two brown gabardines and a rain-cape.
I got to work with thread and kitchen scissors,
cut a length of dowel for wing-struts,
made a balsa wood tail and daubed it in cherry-red shoe polish
with a coat-hanger wire to raise and lower it
and sat in a sycamore three nights in the park.

No luck. The doctor suggested a course of Bjork,
Berkely Square and *Blackbird Singing In The Dead of Night*.
I self-medicated between Axl Rose and Ziggy Stardust
till an episode on a rooftop (it was the herring-gull yodels)
got me sectioned. I absconded without prescription,
nested in copses by ring-roads and flyovers,
quivered gabardine wings in blackthorn winter; lay on
bin-liners inside my wet sleeping bag craving a mic.
One morning I upped sticks holding a sign: 'Nightingale?'
and was dropped off finally somewhere South East
near woods at dusk with my battery running low.

What I heard next was the real thing
as it shook and shocked the darkness awake.
I wrote this:
   'Nightingale with your voice-box, your jewel-box, scattering pearls and opals,
   garnet, beryl, moonstone, carnelian out of the dazzling bush of night -
   no artificer or jeweller can come close'
and left it under a stone on the grass.

I came back next morning to this reply quill-penned
with wet soil: *You a poet? Jug jug jug tereu tereu.*
Then this message woke in me:

> *'No search engine trawling the fetch of the known world will find me; no app*
> *or device command the body of my song as I shudder you now into inner space.'*

I dropped it all as the song began -

others like me shuffled   were gathered   in branches

           taken   shuddering   into the eyes of nightingales

as feathers shrugged and shivered in us   beyond leaves

           imagined wings   tail-bones   out of our beaks

gapes bright yellow   I cannot   cannot   begin

           cannot repeat   explain   what we

           what   we   were   singing   and singing   and

Look At Money

1
Money sets sail on its super-yacht,
flourishes foam and backwash
with a speed-boat in its belly.

Breezes on deck, shoots its cuffs,
sends Piper-Heidsieck champagne-clinks across
continents to summon new bangs for its buck -

high-end ordnance and payloads.

Let money carve into cuts of Kobe beef
for you. See the lavish marbling and the blood
sponged clean with minted new potatoes.

2
Money grunts, strokes calf-skin, conquistador,
caresses with eyes the bombed-out harbour,

fingers with stained bundles down alleyways
the stash of Kalashnikovs and rocket-launchers.

Money drops a lit cigar to set the forest on fire -
watch palm-oil trees and soya sway.

Follow narcotic highways deep into the interior.
Execute a perfect sunset by the boarded-up river.

3
Money breeds money to spawn money
in nuclear flasks labelled *All the Perfumes of Arabia*

Money launders itself clean in our pension funds
which we clutch to our breasts tighter than passports,
shuffling our cards as we wring our hands, lamenting.

We kneel at its altar with innocent faces
as the call goes out for final boarding
in Departures. Belt up. When the jet leans

into its tilt see the gold towers
give us the finger, one after the other.

4
Break into the panic room, escape down the lift-shaft.

Lie tatterdemalion with broken reeds and stalks of maize
in the hang-dog fields. Look at hedge-funds with their threadbare
trouser pockets, their gimcrack leather and eye-holes.

Make a raid on the bank where the wild thyme blows.

The nights grow cold. Tip a suitcase of notes
onto flames to stay alive. A mattress or two.
In the morning sun rakes the embers.

It will fall to sky to water them.

Dazzle, Darken

That look in the soldier's eye,
the way he grips his rifle before the pleading arms

at the checkpoint, the way his Adam's apple dips
as he chews things over

leads from one thing to the next.
It just happened he will say later.

※

The grub of his thought nuzzles from birth
inside the apple - watch it stir, lift a finger,

stare with black-dot eyes until a shell-shocked
building, the smashed ribs of a city

lie flat-out in the morgue. Faces ride
hard trains of thought, carriages slam shut,

histories go bound and sticky, clagged
with skin and bone-glue.

※

Thoughts conjure and multiply in fog,
streetlights flicker through leaves, her heels stumble

as a car's headlamps swoop. Hands reach out,
a door shuts, there is scarcely a cry.

The world has turned to tar at the back of the throat -
nothing we can do will ever get rid of the taste.

Earth buckles under the weight of all these thoughts.
as men lean nonchalantly against the dam-wall. Shrug.

＊

After a day and a night we reach the front of the crowd,
hand over our papers, our precious

stained papers, pray for something to give.
From the same unchanging faces

comes a squirt of tobacco juice; a wink to a superior;
pupils pit dark as olives. Dare we look

up for an instant? *I am begging you.*
There is nothing more we have left to give.

Inside the jaws of what is good and the worst possible
the human animal hunches, quivering.

＊

Dawn might dazzle us with its blessing
at the checkpoint,

gun-barrels move aside, trigger-fingers ease.
We could thank them silently from the depths.

Or maybe not -
will gun-muzzles wake to bark and rip,

hands drag us by the ankles, dump us
hard on the stained metal bed of a truck?

Somehow we are still here,
our hearts running their blind race on the track -

the throat a gag, the tongue a pumice stone.
Gold-leaf or gun-metal?

The heart's bell clangs and clangs.
Our thoughts stampede, leashed with longing.

BRIGHT STAR

Mystic

Agapanthus blue, you open a door to the sea today
and the vase on my windowsill utters words the tide
speaks close to my ear. The warmth of the soil
in the garden listens back, the buzz of a fly
on its wings helps me find words
for the horizon's summer-mirror -

the lobster-fishers in their red boats wake up the bay,
the tern's *skreek* is a pinch of light riding its body
with scissor wings into and out of earthly existence.

I want to explain to you
how the mackerel-shoal that seethes here becomes the chip-pan
in my childhood tended by my father, sizzling as he dips
and lifts its basket to become the sea brimming with life.

We are dipped in this life and come rushing to the surface

with a gasp.

A Mirror of Stephen Street

1
I see shiny-bald
    thick-necked Mr Metcalfe
        blow smoke-rings

in his braces and white singlet
    rest arms on the dining room table
        as tobacco stains spiral his thoughts

up to the ceiling
    facing the mirror that spins him slowly
        in reflection; ex-police sergeant

lighting one cigarette from another
    the sugar in his tea rotating
        as his wife sets down the tray and reverses

so the mirror lifts itself off the wall
    tipping up years
        in a scatter of back gardens and alleys

cantilevering rooftops and
    chimneystacks until
        starlings pour out - leave aerials twanging -

alight on Miss Darlington's watering can
    that dips to slake the throats of blue
        hydrangeas in No 12.

2
Photographs tremble
    on sideboards and sills in a gospel of tongues.
        O Accrington brick of St Anne's on Sea

Stephen St and Sandhurst Avenue -
   your tarmacked asphalt after rain is perfume.
      Now comes a day of flying ants,

the winged females wriggling through
   paving-cracks under cloud-cover
      summoned by smells of creosote and brick-dust

the seconds wriggling free and pushing up
   to take flight, you cannot keep track
      of their wings -

Auntie Doris pastry-brushing milk across
   a meat and potato pie with its fork holes,
      placing it with oven-gloves on the middle shelf

for Harry Bailey's tea, her lodger -
   this gesture she makes repositioning a hair-grip
      lives fifty years in the mirror -

her laugh between No 7 and No 9
   conjures Ruby the spaniel's bark through walls
      as a cat high-tails it along the fence

composing head and feet into an Egyptian carving
   yawning back to its
      needle-teeth.

3
Mrs Penthall in No 15 dab-combs her white hairdo,
   Harry Bailey straightens his cufflinks,
      the Grews are fly-

ing backwards on their swing
   at No 10 Sandhurst, feet aloft by the Corsican pine:
      Stephen, Natalie, Mike and Nick.

Colin their dad at his black Bechstein in the lounge
    assembles chords with an engineer's touch
        wired to Gershwin, Porter and *Fur Elise*.

Now we are jumping walls in back-alleys
    to feel the ringing travel up
        from foot-sole to jaw-bone

and it is nowhere near bedtime.
    The flick-flack of skipping ropes
        the hiding places of Denno 1-2-3

remember every wall and kerbside;
    the scuff-echoes of footballs and tennis balls
        shuffle sunset between the sycamores.

4
We lusted for Jill D with her hair-flick model looks
    but she cast us adrift in a slipstream of scent:
        In Your Dreams.

Bought a box of Weekend
    for Beverley G but the cellophane somehow opened
        and out fell a montelimar and a chocolate lime.

Our bikes turn circles in the gravel
    by a shuttered bungalow
        to brake-squeals of religious disapproval:

the four Joyce sisters walled and coiled in maidenhood,
    terrier-tongued, wagging sermons of sour lemon
        into our Sunday afternoons,

squirting fly-spray at us through Venetian blinds
    to up-end all fun. We ton up the street
        past the Logans and the Alders -

alight at Gladys U Parker's and press the doorbell -
    she answers in her green floral dress and pince-nez,
        her tortoise nibbling a lettuce leaf.

Here is the statue of her African Prince, Nicodemus:
    six foot of ebony unblinking in the hall's darkness.
        Fur coats huddle together on the coat stand

sniffing the naphthalene that is nowhere now,
    Miss Parker is nowhere now
        but in her Victorian drawing room we walk

across the carpet, touch ornaments and glass cabinets -
    I open one and can take out
        her voice with its Lancashire r's and vowels

her blue eyes
    puzzlingly light and clear
        as she gets ready to speak.

5
But just then the mirror tilts
    to another wall and we are spun
        through rooms and back-gardens again -

dice-shake the houses and out we all tumble
    kicking dried-white dog-dirt, walking on stilts,
        venturing knock-a-door run and chain-tig.

Geoffrey Logan, three years taller, sparks up a *Silk Cut*
    I pinch and inhale, try blowing smoke rings,
        slash up the wall as high as he can.

My dad is sandpapering the gate, my mum is clipping the mock-orange
    (they say I once ate petals from it in my pram).
        Our lawnmower pushes

through stalks of grass years ago
    and now dad dips his brush into the paint tin -
        see that streak on the brick wall

right here? It dripped
    one afternoon and you can still see the mark.
        What kind of blue I ask him

and my father looks right back
    through the mirror and tells me
        it's *royal ultramarine*

as the worlds flashing alongside this one
    lift the lid off the tin
        and make a flying saucer of it

scattering drops and particles
    that swallow-dive with us
        into the great accelerator.

Bright Star

For my mother Eileen 1931 - 2005

1
She lost her nerve,
swerved in front of the bus,
toppled onto the pavement
and the conductor cursed her.

Did she give up her Raleigh bike for good?
That's not how I choose to recall it.
Let's say she fixed the oily chain,
dusted herself off,

sped away down the promenade,
bought a racer with drop handlebars
and a pointy saddle,
held time-trials sprinting

to Pontin's head down,
gave us half a mile start
and could still reach Blackpool Tower
with a seagull's feather to spare.

Say all weathers my mother swam lengths
in the blue Lido of St. Annes
and liked her sea-water cold:
The Gazette headlined her the human torpedo

in her scarlet swimming cap and aviator goggles.
She'd back-flip off the diving board
just because she could. Climb up again
to execute a half-twist with pike. Spa-doosh.

Say I asked for two flakes in my Ninety-Nine
she'd let me; would buy my sister a Sky-ray lolly
followed by a Raspberry Mivvi.
She'd neck Babycham straight from the bottle

with a Dubonnet-and-soda chaser,
chuck her empties into the flowerbeds
and challenge us to the long burp. As if.
As if it wasn't epilepsy

toppled her face down unconscious in the road that night
while a gully of rain streamed down the hill.
How she hated it when an ambulance came.
Let's say she was Inspector of Works

peering into a grid to release the flow -
she was public-spirited that way.
Lift her up. Kick these bright puddles of water
away into the night for her!

2
Twice-widowed thrice-risen
she lent us the warmth of her blood and her shelter.
Can we ever repay her?

Forgive the too many capsules
she swallowed that day:
say they were liquorice torpedoes, tic-tacs and imps

not diazepam and phenobarbitone -
fruit polos and wine gums
not a blister-pack of paracetamol.

She phoned the ambulance straightaway
while we were at school, said it would never happen
again. Brave mountaineer,

she scaled the years with Brillo pads for snow-shoes,
faced down the meter and the gas bill,
wrestled damp laundry and the Pifco iron,

headed straight into the teeth of the gale
to sing *Born Free* by Matt Munro.
She fought many a lion in the savannah of her loneliness.

Never learnt to swim or drive a car
but rode the Waltzer spinning inside her head,
squeezed her eyes shut as the sparks leapt again -

you have no idea of what roar and fangs -
the whole Wurlitzer grotesque.
She put her shield around us.

This morning she looked at me through the mirror,
opened the window to tell me about her new life -

done with darning holes in the socks of the Universe,
stitching our name-labels on the night sky

she's steering a runaway train to safety,
   slaloming on powder-snow,
      racing a Pontiac from Paris to Dakar,
         riding a dromedary across the Gobi desert,
            wing-woman to Amelia Earhart on the magic carpet.

      Unwrap galaxies and The Milky Way for her - she is flying.

Signals

In memory of Geoffrey Atkinson 1923 - 2021
RN wireless operator 1941 - 45

My uncle has come back from the other world -
he opens the tea caddy,
pinches between finger and thumb
the lid of the teapot as light streams
from tap to kettle and together we click on the switch.

My uncle is working Cherry Red shoe-polish
into his brogues,
he passes me the tin, poised as he is
above his chair. He reaches
to smooth that tuft of hair again.

His palm rides along the banisters,
clinks and slides coat-hangers in the wardrobe:
jackets, shirts, ties, sigh, a sweater
padded at shoulder and elbow beds in,
a canister of shaving foam jumps back into the mirror.

Downstairs the painting of Holy Island
lies stranded on the tide,
the stool my grandmother carved
is floating in the ebb of the wall-clock,
the books with his prints all over them will go to Africa.

Such things his presence wakes in
feel like Pangea and Gondwana on the move:
the stereogram, the Bechstein piano,
the box-sets of LP's, a picture of Dove Cottage
face down in the sand.

*

Now he moves his fingers in the soil
of the other world,
secateurs snip thin air
for the roses that need dead-heading.
He is tapping his 21 year old self

into morse-code patterns
in the wireless room
of the long-past and here-to-come
as hundreds of ships rendezvous
off St Catherine's Point,

his minesweeper *Damsay*
carried alongside them in the flotilla.
They anchor off Gold Beach
as the barrage starts
at dawn on D-Day -

the battleship *USS Texas*
on his port bow
unleashes a fusillade
that lifts his little craft *whumpf*
with the pressure of each shell's velocity.

*

A still silent wind is pouring through the house -

you held all this in place for sixty years:
a life, a child, a wife, a desk at the Min of Ag & Fish.
You were steadiness, integrity, personified;
three years shy, I thought you'd easily make
a hundred. How neat your correspondence in the bureau.

Now a window opens and a rug lifts,
a harmonic inside the piano
sounds but no string has been plucked.
A glance at this cut-glass bowl on the table
triggers a sun-slapped wave out in the Hebrides -

seventy years after the war
you are sitting on the Uist ferry
and an onlooker remarks he's rarely seen anyone
look so happy. Mountains dip and bob on the horizon,
terns glint their intelligence.

Once on watch at Loch Erribol,
you felt the presence of God
in moonlight streaming across the water.
I wish we could have spoken about that.
Let me into your thoughts again,

let us believe you haven't quite left.
Your eyes blink behind round glasses
towards something else - what is it?
All our chatter now is just interference
between frequencies:

the new stations you are dialling into.

SEVEN PATHS

Listen

Exmoor Almanac

The dipper that afternoon by the Exe
    threaded a high necklace of song above the river's onrush.

Dived in and re-emerged, shaking its wings clear of the water,
    sang once more, blink of silver in its eyelid.

The first blackbird flirting sotto voce with Spring
    makes radio-contact out of holly and ivy

and the song-thrush fashions small ivory statues
    in triplets that echo in Withypool churchyard.

From burnt-out bracken in a hailstorm
    the wren has become a tight bobbin of song, a spinning jenny.

Snow banks deep over the sunless combes and high roads,
    a buzzard plucks mews out of the gut-taut air,

raven and carrion crow with their dark *sprach*
    press down hard on the black keys - snow-fever chatter

of fieldfares and redwing in the fields of ice. One morning
    wind swings west till a chiffchaff, then another,

hang their abacus of notes along the Haddeo and Horner.
    On Preyway Meads the planetary calls of golden plover

meet the first larks high up drizzling balsam from the gods -
    jitterbug of Dartford warblers on North Hill, stone-tap of stonechat.

From branches in back gardens a willow warbler lets
    slip a yellow lace scarf of sound that drifts out towards the Punchbowl

as blackbirds delve deeper into their arias, their coloratura,
   poetic champions composing variations time cannot catch.

One dawn, on the whim of a trade wind, a cuckoo at Three Combes Foot
   arrives, distilling spring and summer into its beech theatre:

two notes, older than the barrows, older than Caratacus Stone -
   cuckoo the ventriloquist popping coconut-heat in the gorse,

conjurer with his cackle as cumulus sail their time-pieces across
   the blue and tree-pipits all morning parachute their song

above Barle valley woods with their dynasties of lichen.
   Pied flycatcher, redstart and wood warbler make vocal the light on water,

Chetsford clings to its whinchats, Tom's Hill its tail-flicking wheatear.
   Nightjar, puckeridge with his moth-frequencies, churrs at dusk

above Ley Hill, tuning the moon's radio-set along a branch at nightfall.
   Silent August rounds robins up to light the first braziers

of autumn; the dipper sewing its silver again by the river
   as if all this could never cease.

Seven Paths to the Visible Garden

For Sue and Tony

I
The blackbird, the muezzin
calls the evening garden to prayer.
We kneel facing west,
our knees stained with sap.

II
Follow the fingerpost of sun
to the copse of wild garlic:
its thick sweet bitterness
lighting a Milky Way
into the dusk.

III
We meet the ghosts of ourselves
playing cards at the table on the lawn.
Open a bottle of Sancerre
with its notes of goldfinch
and distant song thrush.
Long-stemmed flutes
chink to the ice
in a shiver of fruition.

IV
Passengers are waving
from the train whose tracks
once ran across this field.
Under the stone bridge
came the rolling stock
and vanished into these acres.
The stokers are shovelling time -
the smoke from their engines
disperses a million lost thoughts
like giant dandelion clocks.

V

Plunge your spoon into this apple blossom:
junket of raspberry and cream,
cinnamon at the calyx.

VI

Emissaries of yellow archangel
follow the trade routes
over the tide of the lawn.
Is this yellow self-made
or bartered with the butter of cowslips?
Globe-flowers near the picket gate
hold their counsel -
viziers of the original gold.

VII

In this illuminated Book of Hours
the calligraphy
from flower to scent to blade
synaestheses with wing-beat
and *coo-roo* of wood pigeon.
Sun, only you are craftsman enough
to apply such late touches of gold leaf
as if by Appointment.

VIII

The eightfold path
is followed with eyes shut
kindled by the inner flame of the iris.
Open your eyes and what becomes visible?
This tub of ballerina tulips
blood-orange, as the sun
slips easily
down the throat of the horizon.

Exmoor Love Song

May 17th - for Jane

That day is the smallest footnote
in the chapter of these woods.
We caught only a few words

from the minds of the trees
blowing their gift
along the river in meditation

as you waited by the depth
of water and salmon hung
their stillness and flow and clarity.

You taught me to study more closely
what comes alive beneath the surface,
I taught you the calls

of wood-warbler and redstart,
pied flycatcher and dipper,
flitting like librarians

over the water
down the green aisles and colonnades.
Cloud-forest

billowing down these slopes
let us into your library
as long as we live,

speak to us in tongues
so we might remember a line or two
from your books of knowledge,

translate phloem and xylem
sap and cambium
into life and more life

down the sun's spiral staircase.

This blink of coins
we threw for luck
into the Dane's Brook

twirls its small fortune
head to tail

to touch
the Barle
with light.

Infinity Pool at Polpeor Cove

For Iain McGilchrist, author of 'The Master and his Emissary'

In the flood tide just beginning
there are clocks of ripples
in the pools among the rocks,

a heat-struck, wave-set rhythm of breathing
swaying the bladder-wrack back and forth,
scattering works of light in the zawns:

turquoise, aquamarine, cobalt, lazuli,
the miles of energy field out there
where yachts graze

and you are simultaneously on deck
far out in the blue
and on the turf of this inlet

watching the instant of what's happening
                  in its depth of becoming.

Pathways open to the shipping lanes
as memories from childhood surface:
sun one afternoon that shone its galleries of light

through train carriages
turning a bend on the track
as time left your body for seconds

to the world it was first born into -
which is the pulse of this sea now:
a translucent intelligence

beyond the grove of tamarisk -
rise and fall and a catching of breath
as oars dip and glint their water-lights.

The vermilion calls of oystercatchers
ignite lapis lazuli, faience and Atlantic blue.

Alcazar

Gardens of the Moorish Palace

1
The lizard that drinks at the fountain
        slinks from shadows like fragments of lightning.

The unseen cartographers are drawing the sun's maps -
        they crease and fold the walls like parchment

showing us a jewelled fly in the iris of a lotus,
        ingots floating their light across the pool.

A silver arc from the mouth of a stone fish
        pours water in a ring of bubbles, clasping thought

as a kingfisher sparks a heartbeat
        from an atom of turquoise

awaking the tulip tree, the handkerchief tree, the long braids
        of bougainvillea tumbling a drawer of reflections.

2
A mirror flings the sky open
        letting the earth float up as I look upside down.

The nib of a swallow lifts jewels
        of water from the surface, some spill -

its red throat is plumage but might also be infra-red -
        no blue to express the zig-zag of light on its back;

at one angle it is a carrier of gold in a knapsack
        bringing the flies of imagination to this time and place,

with another it twirls a colour-wheel and dissolves
the orange carp reflected in the blue of jacaranda

the way the spears of the palm trees unsheathe their scabbards of light
in a zig-zag motion so that thought becomes movement

reflecting the garden, buoyed up in peace
in the awe of water.

3
Lizard, my hand rests
near yours as you drink at the fountain -

we share the same air as our throats pulse in and out.
The world grinds its gears,

wrong thoughts scalp the tar-sands, jets with their weeping
needles sew up the sky's eye-lids.

Lizard, lend me a flicker of your lightning,
show me paths you take

to the invisible gardens that sing
in the dark.

The Beach University

For Ste - oldest friend, musician, painter, potter, graduate of the Ribble estuary.

Sky casts its bread of light on the water

      kow-yow of gulls on updraft miles out

Peets Light   North Blinker   Horse Bank   The Mousehole

Mullet Man's outboard idles there
      casting a shrimp-net on the ebb -

distance makes a birthing room
      as sea-bass jump with a slap we hear in memory

sensing the pull of the cord.

Turn over and begin
you have one hour this lifetime till the tide turns

says a voice out of the
phoenician-blue

sun-warmed bath
of a mussel shell

      *

The buoyant flight
of quill-pen *skreeking* terns

plunges with entry-dives
into finis terre
      ultima thule

chasing the year's biggest tide -

sand-eels stack
the jeweller's trays of waves -

piece together tales of the hermit crab,
the sprint of the sanderling, the sun's pour of quicksilver

track the redshank's zig-zag to express
this marine-tang of shellfish   umbilicus of water

show all your workings

says the ghost of a cloud
rubbed clean by words

                        *

The wind rifles the pools then mirror-plates them
takes snapshots of your life

sea sieves light
trawls light
is herring-boned with light

something is happening
inside a body of light

that recalls the egg
touched with light

                        ❋

Fluke your anchor high on the sand

these deep-pooled channels are called mulgrums

a hundred oystercatchers klaxon *kleep-kleeps* without cease

that distant red buoy is Salter's
high and dry on the year's biggest ebb -
once you ran full-tilt across the bank to touch it
before the tide fired its gun
on a hair-trigger race
of all beginnings and endings

❊

Take off boots and socks,
wade thigh-deep
in the incontrovertible fact
that the sea braids the current this far out -
she cuffs her cubs, she chides her children,
she will tumble and reef-knot your body
and dump you at dawn
like sodden rope.

A seagull leaving wet footprints
walks up to inspect you.
Tilts its head. Pecks.

❊

If this beach were a religion
its icons would be
the glyph of a million sand-casts,
this sucking wobble of quicksand,
a crucifix made by these criss-crossing jets -
and all of the above.

❊

From Peets Light on its pitch-pine frame
watch a seal haul up one morning.
Using bare foot-soles only
express the wingbeat of each flipper
and the shape it leaves there
shuffling back to the channel.

Make a seal from a ream of clay
dug up from the training wall,
fire it overnight in the kiln.
Next morning, cool and lift carefully.
The sun leaning into its treadle-wheel
will remember you for this.

*

Where do our sons and daughters come from?
cries the curlew playing its cor-anglais
to the North wind

❀

Ocean-prisms split light
into a thousand St Anne's recollections:
ping of the bell at The Cream Door -
(echo-note of Nelson's buoy-bell) -
Sumerian back-alleys of Allenby Rd,
Hope Street, St Alban's Rec,
hot batter through newsprint wrappings
from Cross Street chippy , the salt tang of vinegar;
crystallized fruit on a cake in Kember's,
Keal's tobacconists, the alley down Wally's Café,
Babylonian relic of the cycle stand outside Heap's Post Office,
smell of Holland House tobacco
like soft shredded wheat crumbling in your fingers,
the spiral steps down Galeria Italia,
Blezard's Outfitters and Edmonson's
all swallowed into the ocean.

Gull-throats gulp dawn and sunset,
plane-engines wind down at Blackpool airport,
light bronze-domes the Christian Science church,
capturing the smell of linseed oil and cadmium on your canvas -

the squeak of the swing rocking above No 10's sandpit,
the touch of red lead dust in the palm of your hand,
the weight of keys on your dad's Bechstein piano
lift off a lid and tumble you
into the scent of its interior -
the soft thud of hammers,
the creaking vibrato pedal;
the same note as a seagull's keening,
as it angles wings over the pier
to plane light into harmonics again.

*

Ultra-sound breathes at the tide's turn:
flounder and dogfish stir,
piddock and razorshells lift,
cockles open their hinged *wunderkabinets*
in the sea's kitchen,
funky sandhoppers with their spry tunes
rub grains of sand against each other
as spartina grass sings
older than humankind

little starfish hands
sea-horse mouths
pearl-breaths of water.

You have five minutes
this lifetime
to check your answers,
haul in, sieve and peel shrimps from the net,
fire up the boiler,

says the invigilator, the current,
pressing a stopwatch.

           ❉

With a clap of wings the results are in -

Mullet Man, give gratitude for blue and the mare's-tails
and all the sea-people who came here before -
thank the inventor of the three horse-power engine,
the way it coughs and clears its throat
at the second pull.

This gown of cormorants' wings is fitting,
here is a certificate of light
to hang like smelling salts
in the room of your birth
to revive you -

the hiss of shrimps on the steamer
steeped in your memory
one lifetime to the next.

           *

The rain's press lowers
redshank shiver upwind

high water summons a headache
and the cold tourniquets
your wrists -
           questions swirl
in the belly of the boat.

No end to the booming
of the mind of God across hemispheres.

This beach is the enormous body of God,
her ribs and backbone reach everywhere.

She dreamt up time to befriend her.

Catch her drift
before she calls us all back in.

How With This Rage Shall Beauty Hold A Plea?

For Robin Wall Kimmerer, author of 'Braiding Sweetgrass'.

On hearing the UK government's decision to approve the construction of Sizewell C nuclear power station in Suffolk. The site is next to Minsmere wetlands, a jewel in the crown of UK conservation and one of the RSPB's first reserves.

Shakespeare Sonnet 67   *'How with this rage shall beauty hold a plea*
                           Whose action is no stronger than a flower?'

1
If the day distilled
the Okavango Delta

if the blue
of this sky's savannah

the 100% proof distilled blue
spirit of the horizon

shading to turquoise
the depth of the Ngorongoro Crater

became this Suffolk marsh at dawn -
nothing would be different

to the tribes, this lineage of
reed warblers, sedge warblers, blackcaps, willow warblers,

fast-tongued, jazz-lick Cetti's warblers
taking the lid off the day

with note-explosions in ditches,
grasshopper warblers with their fishing-reel songs,

bitterns blowing across the top of dawn's bottle
as if they were pumping up the reedbeds.

At first light
everything is as it was

when the Jutes first set foot

or the Saxons.

Australopithecus.

2
White noise of reeds hushes. Sun-touch,
splash-ripple commotion of wings.

Bearded reedlings flick
their ball-bearing calls unseen -

nightingales in the blackthorn thicket
wild as action painters

dash off masterpieces of sound.
The cuckoo balances a perfect note

(pig-squeal of a hidden water rail)
like the bubble in a spirit-level,

not forgetting the whimbrel's ululations
bubbling your own larynx

into utterance of a cry.

3
Venus at the diamond point of this chill
lends us a long oar of light to steer by.

There are others who came before us
shawled like the heron whose breath frosts

as its beak opens to the mirror-lake.
Travellers call up the day in tongues

to speak with tench and bream,
tap into the ripple-braille of eels.

　　　　　　　Unbuckle your Amazon
buoyant-winged marsh-harrier!

Fling open your Eastern doors
pochard, teal and garganey!

Pray for the otter's visitation
to part the water's veils

in holy ghost of a mystery!
What a portion of genius silver-bubbling Minsmere dawn is!

4
Each pool makes an altar,
　　　　kneel there. Rub your face in mud. Breathe it in.
　　　　　　Flick holy water. When the shiver down your spine

arrives, pray knee-deep in pond-weed. Fill
　　　　your boots. There are meanings we have forgotten
　　　　　　that the midwife toad decodes for us in croaks.

Egrets preen albs and stoles, their head-dresses,
　　　　the Temminck's stint steals into a pew,
　　　　　　the pratincole bobs, rare as a saint.

This cathedral with its nave of reeds
　　　　tended by avocets and fine-legged stilts
　　　　　　in their black and white robes

lets us dabble in its every religion -
      the congregations of waterfowl,
            rare water-snails and St Mark's fly.

A hide creaks open
      its monastic cell
            for dawn's illuminated manuscripts to take wing.

5

If the day distilled
and the sun refracted its prism
between the reeds,
the eye-beams of others here
before us
would be waiting.

If the life we are living
under the lives we are living
were known as the lark
high up
over gold of the gorse
is known

surely we would
follow its thread?

6
A B C the alphabet says
on screens in labs
in hardcore slabs
while the clicking app of the abacus
the programmed algorithmic fuss
the spread-sheets multiplying digits
conjure the piers the derricks the girders the drill-bits
the steel the rods the diesel tonnage
the tongues of money deep-mining money
the handshake glass-clink-PR footage -

accountants screwing cash out of acreage
from the very seams of the air; chief execs laying bare
with fountain-pen flourishes and a flutter on the FTSE -

the dust-storm earth-heaved crater-depth caterpillar-
tracked bedrock-earthquake arc-lit ur-myth
frack-split head-fuck Hansen-herds
of cement lorries cement-lorries cement-lorries cement-lorries
tip-heavy concrete-mixers pouring the foundations
where the cranes the tallest cranes strut
and cantilever over the country's biggest construction site
the technopolis the radioactive city policed by Geiger
the termites in hard hats
probing calculating testing grasping
determining their dominion.

The grass snake's tongue-antenna flickers.

The nightjar cannot hunt in the drone and the arc-lights.

There are hairline-fractures in the stone-cold eggs of the stone-curlew.

7
How with this rage shall beauty hold a plea
Whose action is no stronger than a flower?

says the flag-iris to the digger, to the marsh-marigold,
the flowering rush, the fritillary and frogbit.

O how shall summer's honey breath hold out?
cries the bee-eater in its harlequin coat from Namibia

where the raw uranium is strip-mined.
Against the wrackful siege of battering days?

yaffles the green woodpecker with its nimble tongue
scrying *The mind's construction on the face of this earth.*

8
If we knelt at a bench of this cathedral and bowed our heads
to hear the aquifers shifting their water-table

took a vow of silence till sign was given
for earth's plates alone to authorise our right to energy

if we could find a way of uniting each impulse
with the meaning underneath the meaning

the breath of awe in the egg we were born from
might find a way to ask the questions:

fuse the grasping mind
with the shiver down the spine:

the lift of the heart
the once-in-a-lifetime

late-remembered
birth-current

opening its vast cathedral
to bow-waves of light

beyond mathematics
and drone co-ordinates

with the wisdom that licks its cubs
tenderly, like the otter.

9
Look into the radioactive seeds of time
and say which grains will grow and which will not

but know what you mean when you say it.

Build bunkers for isotopes in glass,
prison-hulks for a time further off than the Jutes, the Saxons,

tweezer the neutron out of the atom
but ask first

the call of the stone-curlew
face its yellow hieroglyph eye,

the dragonfly aeronaut, the red-footed falcon
lit with the sun's prehistoric crimson.

Ask the brown trout with their sudden splashes in a thunderstorm,
the migrating swifts who taste the wind

and scythe Minsmere reedbeds in hundreds
climbing the Cathedral dome of sky.

Feel this soil in your hands: it is all we have on earth.
Build your Sizewell C next to Minsmere if you must

but not before you ask the non-human people
and wait for their answer.

Why do you talk so much and never listen?
Does the lapwing with its sky-dance,

pwaay-eech i-wip i-wip
give such ultimatums -

the golden plover *puu-pu-peee-oo* in its cryptic flocks
spangling the marsh,

the white-winged black tern
arriving one dawn in a visitation - here then gone -

the Arctic geese
and elvers fresh from the Sargasso?

Do you think earth misses us
because we do not love it any more?

Note
Native American professor of plant biology and elder of the Powatatomi Nation, Robin
Wall Kimmerer, explores in her book Braiding Sweetgrass the compelling idea that not
all persons are human, that we travel this earth with other creatures who collectively
have access to far greater wisdom than we humans do.
The non-human people of this earth throw down a challenge. Their plea? Our
reconnection with all beings. Our freedom is only though consultation and relationship
with everything that lives. This is a direct reference to Native American and other
peoples' lived, practical belief-systems: that humans are not separate from nature, we
are nature. If Sizewell C and Minsmere represent two different ways of looking at the
world, which is the more sustainable?

LOST-LOVE LETTER

Song

It is the hem of a song in a fold of the wind,
in a pocket of air, before the day zips up again, tight-lipped -

a song like the waft of steak
down summer alleyways from a heat-wave kitchen,
the juice of a song melting somewhere into nowhere,
the sweetest sex of saxophone from an open
apartment window before the engines of artics
blast-furnace the street with blue diesel
and sirens burrow through rush hour to the cells and the wards.

It is the first bars of *Say A Little Prayer For Me*
in a Memphis diner, dissolving the stained sugar bowl
and the smell of cheap coffee and grits -
just a taste of the voice of Aretha
marking the intervals between notes on car-horns
segued to plate-scrape and nicotine-clatter of cutlery.

It is the call of the muezzin,
the gull-cry which hits
the chord in A minor of the anchorite;
it is bells through shoals of leaves spinning the wind
into threads of gold for the Abbess at evensong -

micro-tones of the Bulgarian choir, the Indian temple singer,
there are robes this song is wearing and this is how the heart thinks.

Pastora Pavon, Lorca's flamenco *duende*
slugs a glass of fire-water brandy in a Cadiz tavern:
the flame that burns in her throat lights a torch
out of the dark caverns of Franco and the smoke of Guernica -

Amazing Grace swells as the protestors head across the bridge
facing the water cannon and gunshots -

this song attempts open heart surgery
in dark corridors, at the funerals of children,
it pulls its wires through Columbine, Orlando, Uvalde

works deep tissue in the cells,
shakes us again and again
until it snatches our breath

we are crying, we don't know why
we are just wavelengths in far off ocean

Lost-Love Letter

Your boat sheared its wake
across the waters of the loch,
the prop screws churned inside it,
a tang of marine diesel
summoning ripples of my panic.

There are mountains in the mirror-lake,
my telekinesis moves you only further
away. I set off, I search for you
in all the inlets and sea-ports, my thoughts
seething like sea-lice in the cages

of fish farms. I head inland, I find a road
I find a motorway through the glen
I plug myself into the transport network
of your kingdom, I am foot to the floor
but I meet only hold-ups.

I send a search party through the lowlands
but there is no word of you in the fields
only the phosphate like talc in the run-off of soil -
I slip into the river with its foam,
I try a length but it's too cold -

the taste of your silage splitting its bags
cuts like the finger you
put across your throat to tell me
it was all over and would I please stop bleating
about what had been decided?

2
There are fires on the moors, the moon sways
I roam High Peak then the Pennines
North, South, where to head?
East, West, which is best?

I escape to the Lake District.
it zig-zags me
down Harter Fell, snakes-and-ladders me
back to Sellafield -
the slabs of Thorp rear up like Alpha and Omega -

I go back to the truth of us
in our bed of harebells and water-meadows,
we wound cowslips and cuckoo-flowers
there was a freshet
joining ragged-robin and the green-winged orchid -

but I am a railway cutting
where your train doesn't stop,
I am a signalman in fog
hurtling over rails
where HS2 lays its track-bed

I am the ghost of a valley where
your words these last weeks
come back to me as chainsaws
ripping open the path of progress;
a spray-boom of chemicals
drenching hard-core and ballast -

3

- we bedded in the chalk downs
where stone-curlews call
touched the declivities of Exmoor
lingered at the haunch of Quantock

we used to say our children
would be talked about by the nightingales
on Cranborne Chase,
we were Mother Carey's chickens
clucking on Skomer,
Scillies in tryst with Assynt
as the sea scatters its jewels

4

Now I am lost in your arterial spurs
and industrial estates, your distribution centres.
I head down aisles dragging my trolley,
all the night shift I scratch my arms
till the routeways are weals -
with each point of the compass
carve a map of this country's road network
on my body, taste the metal,
my thoughts the blades of gulls at dawn
stabbing landfill.

Your going sheared a wake in the true waters
we once swam in,
how could you fly a flag for these factory ships
dragging their booms on the seabed
how could you have let slip this slick

where no dolphins click, that fills the seaboard
and laps at the lochs? From Caithness
to Cape Cornwall I am grieving can't you see
my mind a-whirl

rocking like Sandettie Light Vessel Automatic

clinging to fallen spars, to tarry sand

to fuck-all at Rockall.

Mother Carey's chickens - a folk name for the storm petrel.

Street Angel

1
It is a dream we cannot wake from
spinning us into a city backyard
as washing beats its wings on the line

flinging a t-shirt printed *'The Road to Emmaus'*
over a bin-lid clattering in the gust. The same sound
a pick-up truck makes as its tail-gate rocks

riding a pothole to panic its cargo of doves.
Their wicker basket creaks and rocks,
springs open in a commotion of wings -

two red eyes of a fantail blink and catapult us
over chimneyed roofs until we are high up,
all fingers and thumbs in the aerial runway of wires.

A junction of traffic lights blinks wide-eyed,
a sudden tower block, three lanes of queue,
a crossroads throbbing, a city on its planes.

2
V on V of fantails' wings claps again -
clocks the peregrine falcon on a balcony,
its roosting head tucked in, its yellow cere like wax -

were we hawks or doves once? We reach the edge
of the multi-storey, that haunted ledge where
the current pulls people back or sends them sparking

into blue electricity. *How come we know this place?*
It feels like the pavement's rushing up to meet us.
I offer you a drag of my cigarette, we link arms

and step into thin air, to sheer *lift:* no gantry
or gutter, no gable, no satellite on its crook of rust
escapes us as we scythe a vent of steam, plunge

over alleys of dog-mess and groundsel, catch glints of
foil near discarded needles under a sudden evening sky
pulsing orange and turquoise, each building below us

shooting up as it wears without consequence
the tiaras of streetlights, taps the circuit-board with
a million thoughts to spark the dirty mind of this city.

3
Super-fast cable at the speed of light
wings past *Ishtar Taxis* and *The Taste of Canaan.*
Then we are kneeling or is it just me

beside people hunched in doorways, wrapped in their cardboard
and sleeping bags, dreaming mothers to cradle them.
Who laid down this concrete orphanage?

Punch the black eye of the night and stitch it with stars
With that you've gone or become someone else
turning away in his dream, your calloused heels

and soles the only bit the child in you remembers.
I lean against a pillar to take it all in, my shoulders
tightening; I crouch carefully beside another

whose nested hair I smell,
whose orange juice rocks in its film in the bottle.
Tiredness in each cell uncurls his hand and grips again -

did he leave his ordinary house with clothes still wet
from the line, the curtains flapping, his hold-all
unzipped? Did a bin-lid clatter and trip as the door un-

-hinged and his charger tore from its socket? I see the
scorch-mark on his face and think of my mother putting
ointment of gentian violet on my oven-burnt arm years ago.

What if all of us gathered here
were looking for a dressing station behind the lines.
What if I were him? Jets tug their needles through the afterglow.

4
Night unrolls its length of bandage:
now I am gravel in the tyres of Range Rovers,
CCTV i-spying the driveways

of gated communities. My thoughts scroll
across immaculate sofas, go blue-lit on screens in bedrooms,
we spiral over estates, the dew-brushed parks and patios -

moths eddy at streetlights to tap the bruise this night spreads
over wet lawns: wounds dabbed and salved with petrol.
Someone hawks up a song, it lies there glistening

as the sodium glow snakes us down-river in a time-lapse
of passageways wired with drum'n'bass, whip-crack snares,
door-slams, dog-barks, deals struck with fist-bumps

that come together and vanish. Now the canal rears up
in a hiss of swans, night presses in
beating hidden wings, a shirt of many questions

burns on my back leaving a scar I cannot touch as traffic
approaches with its calvary of headlights, nailing us
to the edge of the known world. Hold your nerve I say,

follow the trail of broken glass, the smell of melting wires,
our escape is getting closer. In the cross-hairs of seconds
we'll find tickets for a getaway.

Beyond the hard stare of what is actual,
deep in the cracks of pavements,
the gravel wakes.

5

In the underground station a presence approached
we had no name for. A cleaner working on the platform
turned us to face the rails and something we'd always known

stirred inside us. The tunnel-mouth with its smell was real
and the hum of her machine as it moved back and forth
over spat-out gum; now she sweeps past billboards

with their wrinkled skin, fronts the jumped-up tannoy of money
sharpening its talons, stands her ground and we stand
beside her. Not the onrush of a train but a dazzlement

of pigeon-wings as a voice singing *Angel Street*
plucks notes from deep inside us. We gave it this name:
The life we are living under the life we are living.

The Sunlight Opens A Psalm

On a visit of young actors in Joshua Sobol's 'Ghetto' to Auschwitz, 2016

What juice bad-mouths the silence,
squeezes the sun's rind empty?

Two cloths
hang on a ripped shelf
above metal pipes and sink
in a stained and grey-walled room.

I see her appear along the wall,
head-down, shaven-headed, dress torn.
Does the light summon
her husband and children
one last time to her,
little ones she bathes and sits on her knee
and dries with soft towels?

Is the piercing of her care
salved even for an instant in these moments
that take her great distances suddenly -
rags of Gethsemane,
torn cloths of Eden?

The tap remembers its gleam:
*'The spring that was spoken of
has never dried up,
hold out your hand,
put this drop to your lips'*

Her husband is suddenly there
on sun-warmed floorboards
in Essen, Deauville,
Krakow, Thessalonika.
He wraps their children

in soft white towels
and the afternoons of their marriage
are all around in the vastness.

The sunlight becomes a scalpel.
She steadies herself against the wall by that sink
just minutes before it happens to her.

Does she look up and see our faces
at the glass years later?
Our guide says:
'They were taken from this room
to the killing wall between Block 10 and block 11
in the courtyard below
and there they were shot.'

The woman passes in front of us
and I see them force her head down,
tie her to face the firing squad
with eyes that have died already.

Bullets utter and rip,
she twists sideways like all the others -
no-one knows her name
or her husband's, or children's
or ever will.
But here she is -
even in this city of the damned
their love did exist.

How warm the skin
as she cradles the tops of their heads,
speaks in nonsense words known only to this family,
dries between toes and puts socks on,
folds soft towels
not these stiff rough cloths
on gun-metal pipes
in this abyss of a room.

Boots stamp echoes in the world's night.

They were mown down in the gardens
of nowhere
                    everywhere
but the sunlight opens a psalm
along the wall this afternoon
and the tears that were torn from her
when all her loves were taken
become the spring that was spoken of
that has never dried up.

Taste it one last time:
this honey she gives them
from a spoon
she will warm
an eternity
in the sun.

Birth-Star

1
Road, I see you shrug
your carriageways and hard shoulders
fuse your spine with the land
in hardcore and barriers

press your foot down hard
like the controlled release of a drug
veering me heedless over white lines
past the blue-white strobe
                              of junction signs

2
Saturn:
    These children were mine
    long before you arrived

    I close in on them
    I'm in your rear-view mirror

    I take them
    bunched with hunger
    trembling

    like you were in your cot

    I thump with my shouting fists
    drumming it into them for good

    I burn your arm with my cigarettes

    tip you crying out at sea

I will jingle the small change of your life
scroll through your history
past each blind spot

feed you Prozac of tarmac
re-tune your radio
to ghost stations -

your lap scalds with my coffee as you brake

what abnormal loads we carry

3
Moon: *Wind down the window and hurl your cup into the night*

    face the carcasses of lorries   love's depots chained and abandoned

    break padlocks   scale fences

    set foot on the surface of a planet no-one was ever harmed by

4
At midnight
I pull up and stow keys,
walk with panel-beaten heart
into the road's asteroid belt -

the booming shudder of surf
                  hammers headlights home

the jaws of the Herschel crater lock tight -
                  a breaker's yard for the laws of nature

the Tarantula Nebula hurls its meteors -
                  spawning a mushroom cloud

Magellan's Cloud turns into a Catherine Wheel -
a maniac shaking a clock

5
Moon: *Stitch the black eye of the night and salve it with stars -*
if you cannot breathe
prise this neutron star open
make this your stand

6
Road that hurtles
what are you doing to me
opening the door
slamming me in
tightening the belt
turning keys in the ignition
snatching the wheel again
to spin me headlong

7
Moon: *Wrench the wheel back*
just as Phobos moon yanks Mars out of orbit -
press your foot to the floor-
jam the brakes on fast -
make this your entry point

8
I vault the barrier

hang in free-fall

enter the plunging river

rip my belt free

wait for air to breathe

                                   bubbles to rise

        haul myself out onto

              this mud and roots

                             stinging stems

    these junction trees.

              Dig up from spoil of earth

                   a star

                             birth-star

Jynxed

Jynx the sorceress made Zeus fall for Io. His wife Hera's revenge was to turn Jynx into a wryneck bird whose head-twists, hisses and contortions suggested magical properties. In Ancient Greece wrynecks were tied to wheel-like charms (Iynxes) and set spinning to foretell the future.

1
Through ghosts of fields
under paved estates
a heifer thunders where orchards were,
comes to a pawing halt in the dark -
the moon-glow of its hide echoes
the lantern-sway of apple blossom.
Io once had a moon to herself
but now she snorts and drools.
Zeus crashes through branches in search of her.

Trapped inside a wryneck
the sorceress Jynx
hisses from a hole in a tree
writhes her head like a temple dancer -
no chance of other answer.
A Jaguar bellows down the drive:
this is Hera's revenge on Zeus.

2
Snake-bird calling
to light up my phone -
conjure for me upon this screen
a text that she will have me back
and all these scattered fragments turn
what's real into not real.

3
My wife's full of dark matter these days -
pendulum-weights, plunge-drops,
her Sim-card conceals chasms
where snakes slough their skins -

I once caught a serpent looking at me
as she sipped coffee;
it tongue-flicked and smiled
as her screen spun its vibrations right there.

If I thought she did not love me
no roof could house my folly.

I scroll through our wedding photos
but she has vacated the room -
hear the ping of a thousand creatures delighting her
across the lounge, up the staircase
onto the divans of our executive home.

My socked feet cross the bedroom carpet
leave hoof-prints at body-heat
trying not to stalk her.

4
But what about Io?
That doe-eyed one returned my look months ago -
she fell for my bait, we trafficked in sticky bluebells,
unwrapped musk, sniffed wild garlic on our fingers.

Hera found out and the Spring blew up.

5
Why is her wedding dress buried in the wardrobe,
who shoved these wedding shoes under the floorboards,
where are the deeds of our house in their strongbox?

Catch yourself smelling the scent of her bathrobe,
touching her phone like a safe locked and loaded,
a war-chest, a briefcase of missile codes.

When did my lies carve such shape-shifting folly
plumbing the shallows, swerving the depths?
When did the heart mistake satin for spandex

spangled with debts? Each wave and the next
make a set. Send a text. Her boss's Jag scrunches
the drive. They kiss. How much longer to death?

6

No cuckoo on our new estate,
only collared doves that mock the Spring.
A cuckold in shorts, I wheel out the rubbish
turn on the oven, warm up each plate,
spin and spin my wedding ring
as abysses start to sing
in the seas of the dishwasher.

Storm out the house to the orchard end
searching for wryneck, the cuckoo's mate,
ignore the kids and the neighbour waving.
Spinning around on a wheel-like charm
Jynx has trapped me and tied me fast.
Hera, love, please talk when I return.
Truth or dare in human form? her silence will say.

7

Desire's an electric friction
just to generate fiction.

Jynx, begetter of this,
is there something in your very nest

makes these serpent-eggs that rock and tap
to crack the human heart?

Angelie

(after Picasso's La Repasseuse: 'Woman Ironing')

The chatelaine and her ward dip
madeleine biscuits into bergamot tea.
Porcelain cups tremble on saucers,

there is the *frou-frou* of petticoats
and the tongue of a King Charles spaniel
licking its lips after scattered crumbs.

The tchipping sparrows dust-bathe,
the roses in the dry gardens make potpourri
and the fountains chandelier upwards.

As I sweep a hank of my hair back
for the hundredth time this morning,
beads of sweat fall from my nose,

and I think thoughts I have not had before:
- *I have become not Angelie but angle-iron
bent rigid with resolve* -

my iron gripped in sweat-stained cloth
pushes its tugboat against the creased waves
over and over and all my sweat is a drop

in the ocean of the chateau's linen
lost as soon as it falls.
Finis. Wiping my

brow with the back of my hand
I do something I have never done before:
in her salon a key lies in a top drawer

and today, as she and her ward take tea with the vigneron
my fingers close on that key. Fearful,
I take the new francs from her dressing table drawer

freshly-printed with their watermarks,
laundered tight in a band:
'Mais Angelie, pense-tu des consequences!'

I will press her face and trifling endearments
deep into white bed-sheets tight at the corners,
press the years of my service till they burn,

press the ache in my arms and all the angles I iron
as a down-payment on my life to come.
From out the kitchen door glimpse me

for a split-second among topiary of yews
across the back lawn, pacing fast
over the hill to the next village and beyond.

Fresh bergamot pours its scent into tea-cups.
The rhythm of my stride is unbending
and I couldn't give a *sou.*

Tumbleweed

i.m. Michael Brecker, jazz saxophonist 1949 - 2007

Another y was coded into your melody:
something out of key
like a bass-line from a neighbouring bandstand
set your fingers, your breathing askew
so the bridge and chorus would not meet
and there was a gap that jack-knifed your back
till a vertebra broke just like that
on stage at the Mount Fuji Jazz Festival.

M.D.S. Myelodysplastic syndrome, the scan said -
your bone marrow had stopped producing healthy blood cells.
You lay wired up in hospital:
'When can I kiss you again?' asked your fourteen year old son.
So ill you could barely practice for more than five minutes at a time -
like a sprinter on your hands and knees
just to make it over the start line,
you who were once the fastest poet-gunslinger up there -
Zen master of velocity,
John Coltrane in your muscle memory.

It was a disease so rare only another Ashkenazi Jew could be a donor:
your daughter Jessica came close, a half match only -
she donated stem-cells for a transplant to take.

August 2006, New York City. You made it back to the studio,
summoned your life, re-tuned its engine,
unleashed a solo on *Tumbleweed*
that sends heatwaves of vapour down the track -

> how could you go so fast with such perfect
> control wrong-footing us with a switch-back side-
> -winder of notes across bar-lines of space and time
> shape-shifter with a coat of ripples we climb on the back of

hurling melodies that fly like assegais from the plumes of a firebird
into thickets of semi and demi-semi-quavers
that dive under the waterfall past the rock face emerge
the other side clinging on for dear sweet life
where death can't keep up you outran him
calling out Listen this is where I am this rock is me
this river that bore me this spilling torrent of notes
I take my first and last breath from -

we are flying there with you still.

May any of us leave a testament like that
choose our time and place to go toe-to-toe with death -

not fight for breath in a crashed car
gasp in the rip a mile from shore
gag on self-pity at the bottom of a bottle
but be alive as you were, taking the stand
in a blaze of righteous anger
to strike a well of pure joy.

Santa Ana tumbleweed
bowls heedless and weightless
down prairie roads
towards the Interstate -

the spinning shape
of your breath
weaves the soul
onto the loom of your body

and misses not one beat, not one note.

Edenfield

'And all this vegetable world appear'd as a sandal on my left foot form'd immortal of precious stones and gold.' Blake:Milton, Book the First

1
She hands me
    the cracked blue egg of a thrush -
        'Keep it together, keep it intact for the journey,'

The girl on her bike,
    she is cycling to Edenfield, a bangle on her ankle,
        down the track past the dunes and the marram-grass hollows -

a tandem she has borrowed -
    she may not have got permission -
        'No waiting here' she says

'climb aboard' and she's furiously pedalling -
    I synch with her rhythm
        on our Raleigh Discovery *Pilgrim*

that hurtles past the tamarisk and aspens
    down the track between the sand-dunes,
        in the onrush of the pedals and the downward push,

past the fledgling and the stillborn
    in the voice of the thrush.
        Our bike vaults trees in a headlong leap -

the egg wrapped tight in my pocket.
    'This is Edenfield' she says as we land on the lawn
        in a skidding brake of wheels -

'This is your education
    escaping the clock of your matriculation.'
        Lifts me to my feet.

2

'Edenfield. A hotel, a care home, a retreat, what is it?'
    We stride across lawns and she flicks a deck of cards:
        the faces of staff and guests at Edenfield appear

like images on a Tarot pack.
    She deals them face up on the lawn's mown nap
        asks me to study and memorise, deadpan as a croupier.

On the lawn they are serving coffee
    from gilt-edged trays with silver service;
        tide pours its precious metal across sandbanks,

riding the estuary for an eternity -
    I concentrate as the sun strikes a gong on the water,
        take a sip of coffee as a gull lands on the table

pirating bullion of shortbread and toppling cups -
    its throat bulges till its beak closes (she is scooping up the cards)
        and wing-beats launch it into spirit again.

3

Now she deals them face-down in a fan:
    'Choose only one but don't think too long
        or who you are now is all you'll ever be'.

I take a card out and in a dealer's rippling flush
    we are all fingers and thumbs in the cool-store underground-
        the taste of her lips as we kiss, the buttons and zips

flick a switch that takes us great distances -
    'I am in you and you are in me' she says
        till the maitre d', jealous, surprises us - snatches

the pack and deals us a bad one -
    conscripts us into chamber-staff pummelling hoovers and dusters
        tightening hospital corners, kneeling with plungers at the lav -

stands us at sinks chiselling baked-on pie crust in Edenfield kitchens,
    shucking dirty water out of tide-scummed bowls,
        fishing for flotsam of toast-slice and egg-whites.

4
'Screw this for a pastime' she says
    and we escape to the safe in reception where our deck has been stashed -
        turns out the combination is our birthdates combined -

for minutes we fling the cards in the air to become whoever we want
    in the cast-list of Edenfield: rich or poor, in sickness and health,
        dowagers and doormen, the blasé and browbeaten,

those who flash the cash and the widow's mite,
    the matinee idols, the sober and the tight,
        the one-night stands, the hoarders

the smugglers-across-borders, the trenchermen,
    the silver-haired con-men and their mind-reader
        girlfriends, those with secrets

we might learn to tell, using dark arts that could break a heart.
    But we hold back, weighing the exquisite pain of the human day
        till the hands of the clock can no longer be prised apart.

I feel their force as she turns to me:
    'I am the conjurer' she says 'Watch me vanish on the lawn'.
        Plum-coloured shadows bruise the sea -

I try persuading her.
    'I know, I know, but kiss the wing'd joy as it flies and all that' -
        and suddenly she mounts the saddle -

5
the blue egg cracks open and her tandem has flown
    while a thrush soars up to the dome of the sky,
        its azure reflected in the sizzling tide

that sings over sandbanks, tugs boats on their ropes,
    pulls for all its life towards me -
        it is agony in the rooms of Edenfield

lit up as from another world.
    The chambers of longing in the hurt of the heart
        incise the soul like Nazca lines:

these glyphs of Edenfield she carved in me
    as time piles its weight of wind on tide.
        Her face stares out from a card she left behind.

I crouch to retrieve it and a salmon leaps within:
    'Be the bridge between worlds', her voice still carries those words -
        I can reach out and there she is

still alive in the current - the scent she wore,
    the time and place when we were all of us:
        green, eighteen, we knew nothing,

knew everything. This I hold on to.
    On the back of the playing card, penned in her hand,
        is a verse I repeat again, make a spell of it:

'And all this world appear'd as a jewel on my left ankle,
    a bicycle form'd immortal of precious stones and gold -
        unbroken links on a chain of light
            through the passage of time to mansions bright'

William Blake Comes Back as an Oak

When he was eight William Blake saw a host of angels in the branches of an oak tree at Peckham Rye. Oak and poet now speak for each other.

I
Land, there is a fold in your shell-shocked shoulder
I love to nuzzle, a scent at your elbow I want to bury

my face in, feel the sap coming off the fields.
Take a deep breath and rip off dressings

to uncover miniature forests -
ghosts in their shock of green, each embryo of a leaf.

Our first wealth is money-spiders,
scores of tiny webs glistening,

pennycress and hearts-ease through flagstones,
the solitary bee, ichneumon wasp

touching the uprooted, headless, nailed-on ones
the stacked and sawn.

Red ants carry grains of warm soil
to feel our phantom limbs.

II
Hills cry out with flashbacks:
the honey-bee's body with its twelve hearts is beating

over the eight-lane highway, red to ultra-violet
soothing the sonic boom, the crazed sky,

hushing the street-child's tinnitus.
Office-screens blur with moth wings,

they *flic-flac* out of magenta buddleia;
the pond-skater transubstantiates steel to water.

III
Roots, haul up your elements,
buds aspire to leaves on my wrists,

catkins lay gloves of pollen on us,
M25 be damned or soothed, Smethwick

and Ironbridge heal your deep-tissue wounds,
your mills and factories splintered with asbestos,

ulcer ponds where egrets now stalk
and emperors buzz wings.

IV
Rain streams down the hanging gardens
of the tower-block, drips maidenhair ferns and ivy,

plants rosebay willow-herb where flames once leapt.
Night's sirens are touched by a peacock's cry, the bell-calls of wild

geese ring and ring their souls over Hackney;
the windscreens of vans grid-locked

at Elephant and Castle beat with the wings
of pearl-bordered fritillaries

that tesselate Tower Hamlets
The green express sprints down the track of oak.

V
Gospel Oak, tune your lute-strings, spin your webs -
cuckoo conjure daybreak over Clapham Common.

Now we can dream chlorophyll into every cell,
wake and squeeze sphagnum moss

into weepings of pure water,
drink it running down our wrists.

Wash our torn branches
in the becks of Lambeth and Soho

sue for peace
in the wild-flower meadows of Heathrow and HS2,

the sunlit passages of the Blackwall Tunnel and Dartford
the amethyst dunes of Deptford and Shoreditch.

VI
The solar wheel of the North Circular
                    roars its tide in the affairs of men.

This Vegetable World has become a vision unto itself.

A fool sees not the same tree a wise man sees.

Wise tree that sees the fool in every man.

VALLEY OF THE KINGS

The Wounds of a Life Head Upstream

By the door of the shed I opened
fifty years ago in a red brick garden,
presences walk not as ghosts on the lawn,

they are living.

In all the chambers of the heart
I did not know till now
how to tell them I was ready

Grains That Catch Fire

For my father Joe Ryan, 1930 - 1972

Life goes on every day
Hearts torn in every way
Ferry 'cross the Mersey
Cause this land's the place I love
But I can't stay

1
A small window of wave-patterned glass
in the breakfast room.

Outside, footsteps on the path
as he comes back from his round.

Steam from the boiling potatoes
tap taps the pan lid,
mince is starting to sizzle.

His jacket folds over a chair
and the table inhales
his postman's cap.

My sister and I try it on -
I can smell it now but cannot
put my finger on it:

hair-grease, arcane corners
of sorting-offices,
elastic of letter-bundles

creases of sweat from his brow.
Its band had imprinted him
after a morning's delivery,

his hair pushed flat like a schoolboy's.
We'd mess it back up for him.
It was high tide -

high pressure was bicycle-pumping
the cumulus
over St Anne's on Sea -

he brought the happy weather with him,
the E.R. crest on his cap
as he skimmed it across the table.

I see him slicing a potato on his plate,
knife between index and third finger,
balancing tinned peas on his fork,

hear the exact tone of his voice,
feel his cheek with its stubble of toast crumbs
we used to run our hands over.

The wooden heirloom farm stool
he did his boots up on
playing back the generations in its grooves.

2
And if the fire was going out
you'd kneel down,
blow into the heat to make light,
stretch a sheet of newspaper across
to let the flames draw
and they would roar behind there,
the newsprint darkening with glow.
If flame tore a hole in it
you'd bundle it back into the fire anyhow,
later warm the backs of your legs
at the open grate and run a bath too hot,
emerge from the steam
steeped in Old Spice and Brylcreem
for your Saturday nights at the Brunswick Club.

3

Once you put a trumpet to your lips at the back door
to call us for dinner - echoes of your Boys' Brigade.
One Saturday you chucked a tea towel

over the chip-pan fire
but it caught alight, bubbling paint up the wall
then made us keep mum.

Years earlier
flames licked the shoe factory where you were working,
air-raid sirens of fire engines
howled inside livid smoke.

My sister and I craned our heads
half a mile down the railway track
to see blue emergency lights strobing the night.

When your face appeared
smiling at the end of the street
it was proof we were blessed.

4

Like the sugar you'd throw onto the fire
you were the Elohim blowing life into dust
on the palms of your hands,
particles breathing awake
in a crackle of sparks
that flare in the oxygen
of these fragments I remember.

That smoke a premonition:
sister of the dust, brother of ash.

It was your heart
that burnt out six years later.

When the curtain snagged on the platform
the music stopped without ceremony
and the coffin headed backwards.
Just the mechanical buzz of the conveyor
that somehow jolted you away
as if death was no longer hidden from us
and we didn't matter anyway.

My thirteen-year old self
scored with thorns
in the rose garden
where they scattered your ashes
watched specks of you
whirl into the soil.

5
Run your fingers through the aftermath -
this fine grey powder with its fugitive warmth
to find a smudge of who you were,
sudden fang of heat inside.

6
The living have blown downwind
in a blaze of sparks.
In this missing person's inquiry
I sense your DNA everywhere

Man thou art dust
And to dust thou shalt return

muttered Father O'Deay
in his yolk-stained cassock
and black scuffed shoes.

7
Dad, I now realise
I have waited fifty years
for you to come down the path
with the sound of your boots, your singing

still searching for your shape at the porthole
of wave-patterned glass.

The window blinked
when I wasn't looking.

How did I miss you?

8
In the postal strike of 1971
you were shop steward at the St Anne's depot -
one of your workmates called round
having walked the streets all night.
You made him tea and a plate of toast
and I saw how much he depended on you
as so many of them did.

The government and those betrayers
who claimed to lead the union
abandoned you to your rounds
with no pay rise, no cut in hours.
Pressed the tip of a hot poker
into your ribs
until it found your heart.

9
From your hospital bed
on our last afternoon
we talked about a place
you once took me to
where horses came to be fed

beside a stream under the trees.
Take me there again.

Remember
the green woodpecker taking off -
our one bird of paradise?

10
A year after you died
I dreamt of you
digging in the garden.
'What does it feel like
now you've come back?'

Folding the soil in
you looked up from your spade
and said something I have always known

and longed for

which woke me

so I forgot.

11
Make peace with the dust
for it can fall no further.
Dad, you were starting to teach me
how the grains catch fire
in the world of the living,
how the blaze of sparks blows downwind
in the breath of the Elohim
simply in the way
you spun and flew me round the rooms
of who I might become one day -
carried me out of the flames
blowing your trumpet,

beat a free man's rhythm on the walls
to leave the Liverpool orphanage
and the slums of Scotland Road behind you,
put your drum-sticks in my hands,
singing *'Give Ireland Back to the Irish'*,
and *'Pink-a-Pank The Moon is Shining'*:

I remember the thread you wound round a bad tooth
and tied the other end to a door handle
which mum slammed shut -
and *Voila!* there was the molar.
You curled French toast into Savoy-style slices,
took pride in whisking a tablecloth
clear of a laden table, glasses and all,
framed your night-school English O Level
and declared on the stage at Butlin's Pwllelli
your ambition to go to Cambridge University;
made faces at Mrs Gaffney
through the window of her hairdressers'
where all the ladies sat under the dryers
laughing back

lifted me up
to sit on your shoulders
and see.

Rails of Silver

In memory of my mother Eileen, 1931 - 2005

My mother's scream has conjured a long line of black ants
that stretches from the back door
up the arms of the
chair
into the open cupboard by the kitchen wall.

I am thirteen.
Inside the cupboard a seethe of black ants storms
the open red jar of strawberry jam.
Ants run up my arms.

I reach into the core of her sobbing
and screw the lid back on.

I am thirteen.
It is a month since my father died.

*

Something is happening in the kitchen.
The chain of command is turning in circles

the flow reversing
like electrons in current

only stray ants now spiralling on the lino

✿

I am playing cricket
and the soul of my dead father is in the bush
where I retrieve the ball.
All afternoon I can go back there and talk to him,

                          reach down
            and return the ball to the game.
                          It is Ashton Gardens, 1972.

                    *

What was a knock is now a thump.
            It seems his death has made it worse.

Not the thud of a bedside cabinet
being shifted
or the accidental tip-back of a chair.
                    It is her, falling in her fits.
My mother is epileptic.

                    *

I would listen, lid screwed tight.
We would find her dead weight, my sister and I,
                    her cheek pressed to the bedroom carpet
                          not to be disturbed.

Watch her eyes like a stunned bird's
                    as she stirs and swallows
                                    with a little gasp.

                    *

We rowed together on the mirror-lake of Windermere
                    rowed in circles
                              three weeks after my father died.
It was her treat, a trip to The Lakes.

Later, at Oxenholme Station,
                    the Edinburgh Express
flayed half the life out of me on the platform
                          as it rocket-screamed over scorching rails.

*

The electric flutter
        of her eyes -
                warning.

She arcs on the sofa and her mouth turns down,
            her right arm makes a tremor on her chest
                as she topples into the table
                    scattering coffee cups, spoons, bowl of
                                                        sugar.

            ✿

Each fit depth-charges me.

They are looking into her meds:
        phenobarbitone for epilepsy
        valium for tranquility
        anti-depressants for equanimity

like dice they rattle and roll
                in her plastic cup.

One day she loaded the dice
            downed them in one,

reloaded and swallowed
reloaded and swallowed
reloaded and swallowed

then rang for an ambulance
while my sister and I were at school.

We didn't go home that night.
The lid screwed tight.

*

Years later, that detonation sends
                    shockwaves into my sleep.
One time she rang to say
          she had fitted the night before during a rain storm,
                    fallen into the gutter and woken
                    as rivulets flowed past her face, drenching her coat.

                              My eyes still fill with that rain.

                    *

1981.
The dice in the cup, the dice in the cup.
          When her second husband, my step-dad, died
                    she downed a new tumbler-full of dice -
                              left the front door unlocked.
My train home was late.
          it was my best friend who found her,
                    he knocked and rang to no answer,
                    opened the door on an instinct
                              and went up the stairs
                                        to find her unconscious,
                                        saved her life.

                    *

Taste of cigarette smoke on the ward:
                    Wesham Mental Hospital.
          Speeded-up ECT ants are pouring into her synapses.

They say it helped -
          but you were Eileen, Morning Star.
                              How could this have happened?

Our seas were mined and depth-charged.

My sister fired back.
She wasn't going to be a victim.

All our grief submerged again
                    loaded with weapons.

                    *

I am rowing in circles around my heart
            I am rowing to get better at rowing
                        rowing to reach you
            I am putting my back into it
            my heart a-thump with how uncertain I feel
                        what little I know
how unripe a soul
            seeking its ballast.

                    *

You protected me and my sister,
        breast-fed us,
            cleaned our cuts and grazes
    tended me when I split my head open, twice,
                never gave me shame when I wet the bed,
        not once, as you wrung out the sheets.
Each day at the sink I heard
                the washing machine and stove hum
off-key with your hidden grief,
        the Sunday smell of roast potatoes
dissolving into *The Nearness of You*
        on Radio 2's BFPO programme.

        Determined to look after my sister and me
each day of your confusion
we were oblivious
        to the stones your grief

hauled about
        and couldn't offload.

                *

2005.
When I think of all the years between
                how my heart is charged.

There is an island now on the mirror-lake
                with your hospital bed on it
                and you lie there.

                I pull my boat up on the shore
                        and sit with you.

The bush where my father spoke is there
                and he is bringing the ball back for me.
        He sits beside her on the bed
                and takes her hand.
                I see their love now
                        has become sacred.

                Now it's my turn.
        How can a man tell his mother
                that he truly loves her
                when he is numb, and broken too.
Not the boy she gave birth to, but the man.
                How can I tell her?

                *

Soon a train will arrive
and stop at her station.
My heart is thumping,
I am polishing all the brass,

varnishing the wooden benches
for her departure,
watering the hanging baskets with tears.
I pace the waiting-room,
I see it bears the livery of the morning star, Eileen.

Behind it lies the pain
of all I could not do for her
all we could not connect
year after year.

I want her to know
she is precious cargo
and the gods on their rails of pure silver
only have love for her.

May a man when there is falling
in a particular time and place
be able to tell his mother
this true thing,
as I do now.

What happens next
is her hand that squeezes mine
then relaxes,
holds it tight and relaxes -

it is something we keep telling each other
in the life still open to us,
smiling.

❋

Afterwards
we row on the lake again
and I take her to places
we have never visited -

islands of mountain-ash,
sunlight flaring on gorse
across a bay of good hope
that ripple waters
before either of us were born.

The oars grow still,
we drop anchor,
the rope tautens
and we reflect on how
we can lift the weight
and lower it again,
feel the pull of the cord
and its release.

May a man and his mother
show their love for each other,
row a boat on a lake
holding its palms wide open
to the forgiving sky.

God brushes
the vastness of the water,
touches both our hands.

The Train

1
There was a window banging all night
that made me leave my room before dawn
and lean onto the ledge in the stone tower
and clasp it shut -
                    but it flew open instead
and I opened my mouth to catch a breath -

the night wind ferried the dark before dawn
into many voices a river of faces -
blew its thoughts into the building
where others like me lay asleep -

between gusts
                    caught my dad spinning
a tray-full of glasses in a dance of spread fingers
in 1950 - grinning with the other waiters
in The Whitewell Hotel at The Trough of Bowland,
his body a frame for pictures on the wind
as he spun my mum at the Nurses' dance,
shook cocktails at the Toby bar
and the letters of O Be Joyful lit up one by one
on the neon sign outside that was rattling
near the station
                    and the no-stopping London to Blackpool train
hurtled its shunts of steam
                    flashing carriage after carriage
and I was standing on the platform and jumped into one,
all the windows of the train turned to face me -

                    if I planted my feet on the carriage floor
pressed my stomach
the pictures could flow in and out
but I couldn't stay upright in the onrush -

119

under the rhythm of the wheels
the train picked up speed
and the voice of my boyhood Catholic priest
pacing the altar on Ash Wednesday

uttered the same words over and over
as he thumbed our foreheads with a dark cross:
Remember man that thou art dust
And unto dust thou shalt return

Grains crumbled on the wind that spoke in tongues
as the train swayed past fields and farmhouses

and slowed so I could jump out stumbling and get my balance -

2
It was a lawn I stood on,
I saw a woman in a fur coat,
my great-grandmother with a necklace of crystal
in diamond-shaped points
above her high-necked dress -
her left hand rested on a chair set on the grass
her five daughters sat around her
and I noticed from my grandmother in the middle
that her mother had second sight,
you could see it in her eyes,
how they narrowed in appraisal like a fox's -
she saw me in the garden and stared at me -

        till it became my mother in her pram
being pushed by *her* mother down Headroomgate Rd
in 1932, sculpted by sunlight and shadow
under the curtains of mock orange blossom
which I would smell from my own pram years later,
the town of red brick glinting
with windows and window-shoppers,
motor cars exhaling at the sand-dunes.

120

                    The air turned its needle west
and the train returned,
I swayed out into the wind of it down the platform,
leaned out more till the urge in the centre of my stomach
merged with the onrush of the express
and I was off into a gulp of air -

a pool spooled open
the way a tide snakes across sand
pushing its ripples into ridges and wave-bends -

miles away beyond Southport
Great Orme near Llandudno
was a cut-out on the horizon -

then the tilt of the sea and land
                    became the Wicklow mountains
the peat-bogs of Offaly and Tipperary
where dad's ancestors came from
and someone I'd never known
sat crouched in her shawl

near a bogland pool on a tussock of sedge
and turned to face me

a look I wish I'd never seen -

too late to turn away
I knew what her eyes and mouth foretold

in the sky-shimmer
and quiver-full of rushes
the midge-bites and blur of bog-cotton.

Larks wrung their songs in the drizzling air
carrying the baby-cry of the curlew, the whaup -

she said *an chrotaigh*   *the curlew cried her eyes out*
chaoin se uisce a chinn

flying dark crossed wings
into the future -

3
Which made landfall
in Liverpool
seventy years later as my dad aged seven
with his elder brother John
pushed open the back door to the tenement
smelling gas-fumes in the kitchen
and found my grandmother slumped by the door
of the hissing unlit oven,
the granny I never knew,
left with six kids when her husband walked out:
John and Joe, Winifred and Mary, Tom and Roger.
She slipped away from them that afternoon
down and down into darkness so far away
beneath the street-sounds of the Scotland Rd,
the skipping-games and football, knock-a-door-run,
the bootsteps on flagstones, cart-hooves, motor-cars.
She was Ada.
There exists no trace of her, not even a photograph.

She sealed time in that afternoon
wound her children tight in their shrouds
as from ancient Egypt
never to be unwrapped.

I stand with my torch
in the tomb of that kitchen
as at the womb-entrance
never to be opened in my lifetime
and the soul's contractions
fix forever in their patterns
like ammonites in the rock.

Lift her head out of the oven,
cradle it in your lap, hold her close as you can,
the ambulance men will lay her body on the stretcher
and the orphanage open its doors for her children.

Dad I will take your hand
and lead you from that room
floored with stone in your memory
where the milk-pan burns its skin,
the tins and packets lie half-open on shelves

and the loaf in the pantry with its half-life
scatters its crumbs
on a hissing sea that time circles
as she turns on the gas again -
pictures he cannot un-imagine -
and puts her head on the stained metal shelf
she has no pillow for
while silence fills her mouth.

Dad I will hold you close
only my mother will tell me your story -
the one time I saw you cry was when you
spoke of a stray dog
you found in a back street
near the docks
before all this happened
and you played with it on your way home
but they wouldn't let you keep it, you had to let it go.
You are both that boy and the dog looking back at you
as you turn the corner
and a wave of the sea breaks inside us
never to be named in this lifetime -

4

      Into and out of the birth canal,
where the wind through all points turns
and the needle's quiver settles.
I am standing on the train platform
opening my mouth to catch my breath.

      Thoughts arrow past
carrying my mother smiling from the open window,
her father Willy Atkinson in his shirtsleeves
with his arm round her and a pipe in his mouth
drawing on his one good lung
after he was gassed near Amiens in 1917.

Beside her is the woman who stood by that chair on the lawn
my great grandmother, the one with second sight

as she channels it through that crystal necklace
and then gives it to my grandma, her daughter,
who reads my uncle's morse and sonar
from the minesweeper *Damsay*
moored off Gold beach on D-Day
and simultaneously sees him safe at the foot of her bed
as he is writes her a letter from the battlefront -

      There are trains heading to the Channel
there are troop trains crossing this country
with their cargo of souls,
there are carriages that haven't made it yet,
how do you know there aren't ghosts
among the crowds at Euston or Kings Cross
holding a coffee-cup, scrolling through their contacts,
shaking your hand to leave body-heat on your palm,
a ghost playing the piano in St Pancras' concourse,
a song called *'The Living and the Dead Are One -'*

which is the headline on the news-stand in front of me.

There are pictures of our family on the front cover,
my sister sits alongside me and we read it together.

                                                    It says -

'In a time to come you will hear
a window banging in the night
which wakes you still dreaming -

leave your body lying on the bed
and find yourself outside the stone tower
on the station platform
near the bar where your dad pulled pints
after he left the orphanage and the Whitewell Inn.
O Be Joyful
you have work, a lot of work to do
because the wind that got up in the dawn
opens its mouth again to catch your thoughts
and let the pictures out -
you have left it too long -

it is not in your gift now
to slam them shut.'

5
                The express hurtling down that track
swooped an inrush of breath
down the blind tunnel
gathered us up
as we yelled
into stone and darkness

and the sound-wave that hit
vibrated one second too long
in our lungs

became a dazzle of daylight
as our ear-drums burst
                                    out of the tunnel.

6
We gasped for air

light flooded
the open window

people dozed and scrolled
as we swayed down those carriages
that ran by the sea, my sister and I.

'The sun out there, what is it using us for?'
said my grandmother turning cartwheels
my great-grandmother walking on the lawn
waving as the train slowed.

We took our places
on the way to our birthplace,
my other grandmother in the tenement
cradled by hands soft as Jesus'
as he watched her fall from sight
when she slipped from time that afternoon
and my dad and his brother
forced the back door
into that kitchen.

My mum and dad answered:

'Sit and listen to the sun
can you hear it move?
It is recovering the dead
and that is your first wonder.

Look at the fireplace on water,
the window into the workings of the clock,
the blaze of light over the sea's hospital.
A dog is running down the street
heading for home -

if you look through its eyes and let it in
you will see miracles.'

7
                The sun was up.
I went back to my room
and climbed back into my body

which lay on the bed

a garment fit for the time being.

Valley of the Kings

1
He sat there, his gaze neutral,
his right elbow on the table.

He sipped a glass of water and for a
second he had my dad's face, then he didn't.

2
I dipped my finger into grains of sand on the windowsill,
he scooped up a tiny dune, weightless in his palm -

grains on the sloping windscreen of the car, along the wiper-blades,
sleep-dust of sand on the cusp of the door.

3
I understood
it was sand carried on the Levant or the Khamsin wind

and my dad was somehow himself and other:
barman, shoe-fitter, postman, wage-slave

had become a quarrier in the Valley of the Kings,
hewing and tunnelling to make chambers

where Pharoahs could rise and greet the afterlife;
years of hard labour moulding slippers in the factory,

tramping down paths with a mailbag,
had become picks and adzes of a chain-gang in the heat.

4
I blinked
and it was my dad again

taking off his postman's cap, skimming it
through the open door into the living room.

5
'I was a slave for years, pinned down by the constellations,
eyes red from sandstorms, ' he said

'earning a wage for you all,
dust in every line of my palm, stone in every vein.

I went to night school got my English O Level,
got my head round some figures,

left the orphanage of my childhood behind,
I came to tell you something.'

My blink caught his cap before it landed,
I saw his shiny-arsed trousers

as he kneeled at the fireplace
tying spears of newspaper into knots

to light the fire with,
gate-crashing our football game after his afternoon nap.

6
Sand drifted under the door.
My eyes pricked: he was the stone-mason again.

'We sat there' he said, pointing to the wooden bench in the kitchen
'we tied our shoes there most days, your dad and I.'

The dust of them streamed in beams of light from the window -
I remembered Howard Carter in the black and white photos

at the opening of the tomb, motes ascending the sun-shafts.
The mason smiled as if he read me

and then it was my dad again dipping a chip into his fried egg,
blowing across a pint mug of tea as he hummed *'A Hard Day's Night'*.

'Listen' he said. 'I met a mathematician in The Valley,
he had instruments for measuring the sun's height

and azimuth, tracking The Crocodile and Hippo over the desert.
At the end of a long day he opened a door

to the stone-carved corridor between the living and the dead,
lifted a slab, took out a parchment he'd scribed,

said he wanted me to look after it.
It read: *'The lives we could have lived*

have filled up with sand, but is that the whole story?'
My dad looked up at me:

'You, me, your mum, your sister, we were on a track,
then I died, but the path didn't stop, you just can't see it.'

'Our lives took a wrong path!' I cried out,
hot with accusation, deep pitchers unearthed after an age.

He gave me a look which punched me clean in the stomach -
I wanted to get out of my chair and push him back -

I remembered the day he got furious and walloped me
when I'd been so difficult and my sister was ill -

the years blew away in a landslide, the cracked mouth
of stone brimmed with daggers of active shadow.

'I know, I know, it must have felt different to you,
stumbling in the footprints you were forced to make

in a windthrown place, scratching
marks in the sand to steer by.

But we are torn from our stories and must go on,
God's thumb presses us into our shapes again.'

7
Where had I hauled these tears from?
I was a pitcher of weeping, my heart a Canopic jar -

He gave me a cloth to wipe my face:
'A part of you died with me, but -'

'*All* of me died!' I shouted back at him
and at that moment I felt it was true.

'You aren't the first' he replied, what about me, both my parents gone
and six of us, my brothers and sisters, in the children's home?

Somehow you have to link the path you are on now
to the first one in your heartbeat, sprinting down the street,

the first time you rode a bike
and took both feet off the ground.

I was the same, kicking a ball towards goal,
blowing a trumpet at Boys' Brigade, I was born a slave

but I spun you feet first and you laughed your head off,
no dad ever did that for me. Now you've entered the tomb

where I lay that Sunday morning,
and couldn't get up because I was having a heart attack -

this fly on my wrist beats with more life than I can find
to tell you, the glossy ibis on the banks of the river

glows iridescent with all this life,
the Nile perch and catfish mouthing at the womb of life'.

8
'It's not enough!' I cried.
He smiled and laid his hands on me. I froze

and it was as if I was the water-boy
who first spotted the stone steps

under sand leading down to the tomb
in the Valley of the Kings.

I had to run to make everyone pay attention,
say what I had seen or no-one else would follow.

I heaved dumb rock aside under broken fingernails
in the flame of heat to prove what I knew was there.

'That power in that Valley is still yours to discover:
the moon's pull, the weight of the sun, their alignment,

it wakes in you'
and it was my father there absolutely

as if from ten thousand books
in the burnt library of Alexandria

the right page had fallen open.

9
The birthplace slums of his Liverpool
rose up, a light transported us

past dockyards and tenements,
over back-alleys where children hop-scotched

and faces beaten down on the Scotland Rd
squinted into the sun beating in the wings of sail-boats.

A crew heart-strong and nimble with blood.
held up a child crossing the sky,

I stood in the prow of my father's sun-boat
steering the dead and the living.

*'The mound of flame rose out of the waters. The god
in the form of a falcon landed on the mound*

which was the first land' -

10
My father walked towards me,
I watched his footprints filling,

his smile, his quick-bitten fingernails,
his brown hair and eyes, were just the same,

those thin ankles that I had always thought weak
were oars of strength,

I was ashamed I had ever doubted him.
He aimed his love at me

my mind was ablaze.
He was putting robes on me,

he poured us both water
from a stoneware jug

and we drank in its light,
wiped our mouths with the same gesture

as grains suspended
the hour-glass on the table.

An asp of sand
wriggled out of the door.

The desert wind blew itself out
and stilled in peace.

On 4th Nov 1922 a 12 year old water-carrier lodging a water-jug to stay upright in the sand found by chance the first steps leading down to the then undiscovered tomb of Tutenkhamen. His name was Hussein Abdel-Rassoul.

Party at Pigeon Ogo

(A sea-cave in Cornwall)

The spray that plunges
and sashays
at the base of each rock

scatters Bollinger and amethyst
with a *whump* of bass
adds a dash of chartreuse

in fistfuls of mist
turning to rainbows the nebuchadnezzars
and sizzling melchizedeks

from the sea's capacious cellars,
proclaiming *Vyaj sallow!*
to the black-backed gulls

that cork the waves
in bladder-wrack submerge-upsurge -
cables of spume a-sprawl

in a power-play of sun
making tunnels of curves
that the waves glow glass-green -

each crest a kabbalah of light
a jeweller's tray, a wedding
shekhinah.

Today the sun
picks up the tab
and knows much more

than any of us,
so head straight to the bar
most fitting guest

Yvaj sallow!: Cornish for Have a good day.
A Nebuchadnezzar and a Melchizedeck are twenty and forty-size bottles of champagne respectively.
Shekhinah means the presence of God in the Judaic tradition

Acknowledgements and Thanks

The Homeless Man Thinks of Ancient Egypt won 1st prize in the Teignmouth Festival Open Poetry Competition 2018, judged by Pascal Petit.

Ignition won 3rd prize in the Torbay Festival Open Poetry Competition 2017, judged by Penelope Shuttle.

Look at Money was commended in the Teignmouth Festival Open Poetry Competition 2021, judged by Helen Ivory.

To Become A Nightingale and *A Mirror of Stephen St* were published in New Contexts: 1; *Jynxed* and *Song* were published in New Contexts: 2 (both Coverstory *books*).

Thanks to Ian Gouge and Coverstory *books* for your painstaking editing, the generosity of your support and your belief in emerging poets.

Thanks to all at Fire River Poets for your great support, inspiration and forensic skills over the past six years - chapeau!

Thanks to Katie Griffiths for your wonderful poetic inspiration, your open-hearted mentoring and all the confidence you continue to give me in my work.

Thanks to Ama Bolton for your immense affirmation, your generosity, time, and the quality of your reading.

Thanks to Melanie Hall and all our wonderful explorations in *Spirit Matters*.

Thanks to Matt Bryden for all your support and for holding me to the mark.

Thanks to Sue Boyle of Bath Writers and Artists for all the support, creative opportunities and exemplary challenges in the workshops you have led.

Thanks also to Verona, Mo, Peter, Linda, Eileen and Marilyn for your great support and input.

To all at Poetry Teignmouth and the wonderful Poetry Festival you run.

David Niven and the BardWindow poetry website and podcast.

Jacqueline Saphra, Helene Demetriades, Claire Williamson and Moniza Alvi for your generous close readings.

And to my wife Jane - with all my love and thanks.

Notes

The Long Tide - There is a video of the research of a botanist, William Seifriz, on primordial living organisms at the University of Pennsylvania in the 1950's. The slime mould is an undifferentiated fluid mass of protoplasm without cell membranes, and with multiple free-flowing nuclei. Seifriz studied it under microscopes and noted that its protoplasm was constantly streaming first one way and then the other in 50-second cycles. He also noted that this is a stable rhythm, not affected by any toxins and anesthetics he introduced. With great insight, he said that if we could only understand the nature of the constant and stable rhythmic streaming of the protoplasm, we would be close to understanding life itself. He was observing the Long Tide acting directly in a primeval organism and realised that it would underlie the organisation of every living thing - not least ourselves: a dynamic field of action that is continually being renewed and re-established in every moment.

Ignition - the energetic process at the moment of conception. Human life begins with a bright flash of light as a sperm meets an egg. Scientists have video footage showing that at the exact moment of conception an explosion of sparks erupts from the egg.